OUR BELOVED NANA

"ELDORA
FIG
DALRYMPLE"

WRITTEN BY TOMEKA ARTHUR

DEDICATION

MOM, I HAVE BEEN ABLE TO SHARE THE MAJORITY
OF MY GREATEST LIFE JOYS WITH YOU.
YOU HAVE BEEN WHO I HAVE NEEDED
YOU TO BE IN DECISIONS AND IN JOURNEYS.
I USED A SHADE OF YOU FAVORITE
COLOR FOR YOUR LAST BORN GRANDSON'S BOOK,
AS A DEDICATION TO YOU.
I CHOOSE A SHADE OF MY FAVORITE COLOR
AS A DEDICATION OF MY LOVE FOR YOU.

LOVE
YOU WERE VERY YOUNG WHEN YOU
LOST YOUR FIRST TRUE LOVE, YOUR MOM
WITH THAT PAIN I AM GRATEFUL THAT YOU
STILL KNEW HOW TO LOVE
WHEN IT CAME TO YOUR HEALTH
YOUR HEART GAVE US YOUR BIGGEST SCARE
WHEN IT CAME TO LOVE YOUR
HEART GAVE US THE MOST CARE

FAMILY
IT WAS MANY WHO LOVED YOU FAMILY AND FRIENDS
ALIKE YOU LOVED US ALL BACK . YOU WOULD BRING US
TOGETHER TO TALK, LAUGH, PLAY, SING, DANCE, COOK,
CELEBRATE, AND JUST HAVE A GOOD TIME DOING WHAT
WE LIKE TO DO, AND THE NOTES IN THIS BOOK IS JUST
ANOTHER SMALL
TOKEN OF LOVE AND HOW MUCH YOU MEAN TO ME.

FAMILY, LOVE, AND COOKING WILL ALWAYS BE
A PART OF MY LIFE DEDICATION
TO THE WOMAN YOU ARE AND SPOILED ME INTO.

MOM, I LOVE YOU FOREVER AND ALWAYS

TABLE OF CONTENTS

CONVERSATIONS WITH MY MOM...

THE MEMORIES THAT I HAVE OF YOU
WOULD LAST THREE LIFE TIMES
YOUR SPIRIT IS EVER LASTING AND
KEEPS ME FROM CRYING SOMETIMES ...
YOUR GLOW SHINES SO BRIGHT
SO I WILL NEVER NEED ARTIFICIAL LIGHT
IN THE DAY TIME YOUR SOUL
IS RESONATED THROUGH WILD LIFE
YOU ALWAYS TAUGHT US
THAT RED BIRDS BRING GOOD LUCK
AND WE HOLD THAT CLOSE
SO EVERY TIME WE LOOK UP
AND ARE GRACED WITH THE PRESENCE OF ONE ...
WE KNOW THATS YOU
CONTINUING TO FLY OVER US
LOVE U MOM
YOU ARE THE MOST BEAUTIFUL

CONVERSATIONS WITH MY MOM...

AS THE YOUNGEST OF THREE
I WAS BLESSED TO SHARE YOU WITH
MY SISTER AND MY BROTHER
AS WE BEGAN TO HAVE CHILDREN
I SHARED YOU WITH THEM TOO
& THEY WAS GIVEN AN ENORMOUS
AMOUNT OF LOVE AS A NANA WOULD DO
YOU DIDN'T WANT TO BE CALLED
GRANDMA FROM DAY ONE
YOU WANTED TO BE THEIR NANA &
YOU ARE A GREAT ONE
SOME OF OUR CHILDREN CALL YOU THEIR MOM
THAT IS A GREAT GIFT FROM YOU AND
THE IMPACT OF LOVE YOU BLESSED TO THEIR SOUL
THEY LOVED YOU THAT MUCH
CAUSE ONLY A NAME LIKE MOM SIMPLY MEANS LOVE
IT WAS SO MUCH LOVE THAT YOU BECAME OUR NANA
MY SIBLINGS AND ALL OF SPOUSES CALL YOU NANA TOO
AND WE SHARED YOU WITH A COMMUNITY
OF THOSE WHO LOVED YOU TOO
I AM THANKFUL THROUGH THE
GOOD AND BAD THAT YOU LOVED US
THE LORD DID NOT TAKE YOU FROM US
BECAUSE YOU LIVE WITHIN ALL OF US.

CONVERSATIONS WITH MY MOM...

WHEN SHE SMILE, I SMILE
WE SMILE TOGETHER
MOM I AM THANKFUL FOR ANOTHER DAY,
THANKFUL FOR EVERYTHING YOU PREPARED ME FOR.
I OFTEN SAY YOU PREPARED ME FOR EVERYTHING
EXCEPT HOW TO LIVE WITHOUT YOU.
WHEN I CRY, SHE CRY, WE CRY TOGETHER
SHE SHINE, I SHINE, WE SHINE TOGETHER
THE LOVE OF MY MOTHER
YOU WERE ALWAYS A DIFFERENT BREED MOM ...
YOU ARE A PERSON THAT CAN'T BE DEFINED BY WORDS ...
YOUR ACTIONS WERE SOME OF THE REALEST EVER ...
I LOVE YOU FOREVER
THE LOVE OF MY MOTHER
GOD DIDN'T ALLOW YOU TO TRANSITION
BEFORE YOUR TIME.
THE LOVE OF MY MOTHER
I TRY MY BEST TO HOLD YOUR VALUES TRUE
I AM THANKFUL FOR YOU ALLOWING
US TO CALL EACH OTHER FAMILY.
I CAN'T TAKE NO ONE ELSE'S PAIN OR TAKE ANY LOVE
FROM THEM ALL I CAN DO IS TELL MY STORY.
HOW I LOVE MY MOTHER.
HE DIDN'T ALLOW YOU TO COME WITH HIM
UNTIL HE KNEW YOU WAS READY
READY FOR YOU TO TRANSITION INTO THE FULLEST OF
YOU, THE PERFECT YOU, THE PUREST YOU.
MY MOM FOREVER

CONVERSATIONS WITH MY MOM...

MOM AS I SAT WITH YOU, BOTH OF US IN PAIN
ADVOCATED AND GAVE YOUR SPIRITUAL TESTIMONY.
AS A MONTH TO THE DATE PRIOR I NEVER KNEW
WHEN I CAME TO THAT HOSPITAL
A HOSPITAL YOU CHOOSE FOR THE VERY FIRST TIME,
THAT MY HEART WOULD TAKE IT'S HARDEST HIT.
AS YOUR FLESH WOULD NOT EVER BE THE SAME;
I DON'T KNOW HOW MANY TIMES THEY TOLD ME...
MY HEART LITERALLY HAS NOT BEAT THE SAME.
AS THE PAINS IN MY HEART REMAINS.
EVERY TIME YOUR HEART NEGATED IT'S PURPOSE,
MINE DID THE SAME, I TOLD HIM
I WISH I COULD GIVE YOU MINE ...
A MONTH AND THREE DAYS LATER THE PAIN STILL CAME.
THIS TIME IT WOULD NEVER LEAVE,
AS YOU HAD COMPLETED YOUR LAST STEP,
SO I COULD TRANSITION YOU BACK HOME
ALL YOU WANTED TO DO WAS GO HOME
BUT ALL GOD KNEW THAT YOU WAS STILL IN TRANSITION
TRANSITION TO HIS HOME YOUR ETERNAL HOME..
MOM I CAN'T GIVE YOU MY HEART CAUSE
YOU TOOK IT WITH YOU

HAPPY BIRTHDAY ALWAYS MOM
I TRULY MISS YOUR BEING
WE ARE TAUGHT THAT THE HEART IS EQUIVALENT TO LOVE,
SO WHY DOES THE HEART HURT,
STOP WORKING OR IS OFTEN BROKEN?
ONLY IF LOVE CAN KEEP THE HEART STRONG
THROUGH ALL THE EMOTIONS AND DAMAGE.
ALWAYS I LOVE U ..
YOU ARE MY FAVORITE GIRL
MY HEART ACHES FROM YOUR PHYSICAL ABSENCE
YOUR SPIRIT IS PRESENT AROUND US
THANK GOD HE MADE YOU ONE OF MY ANGELS
ON EARTH AND IN THE AIR ...
AND I CAN FEEL YOU NEAR
LOVING AND APPRECIATIVE, IT BRINGS ME JOY
THAT I DID SPOIL YOU WHILE YOU WERE HERE...
I MADE IT MY BUSINESS
TO TRY AND GIVE YOU EVERYTHING
YOU ASKED FOR OVER THE YEARS ...
YOU GAVE ME SO MUCH MORE ...
WHEN YOU WAS AROUND I HAD NO FEAR ...
AS A WOMAN YOU PROTECTED AND LOVED ME ...

YES MOM I KNOW YOU DON'T WANT TO SEE THE TEARS ...
SO MANY TIMES YOU SAID STOP CRYING BABY ..
YOU GONNA MAKE MOMMA CRY ....
MOM YOU SEE OUR PAIN BECAUSE IT WAS YOUR TIME TO
TRANSITION... THE MONTH OF SEPTEMBER
WILL NEVER BE SAME
BECAUSE YOU ARE MISSING

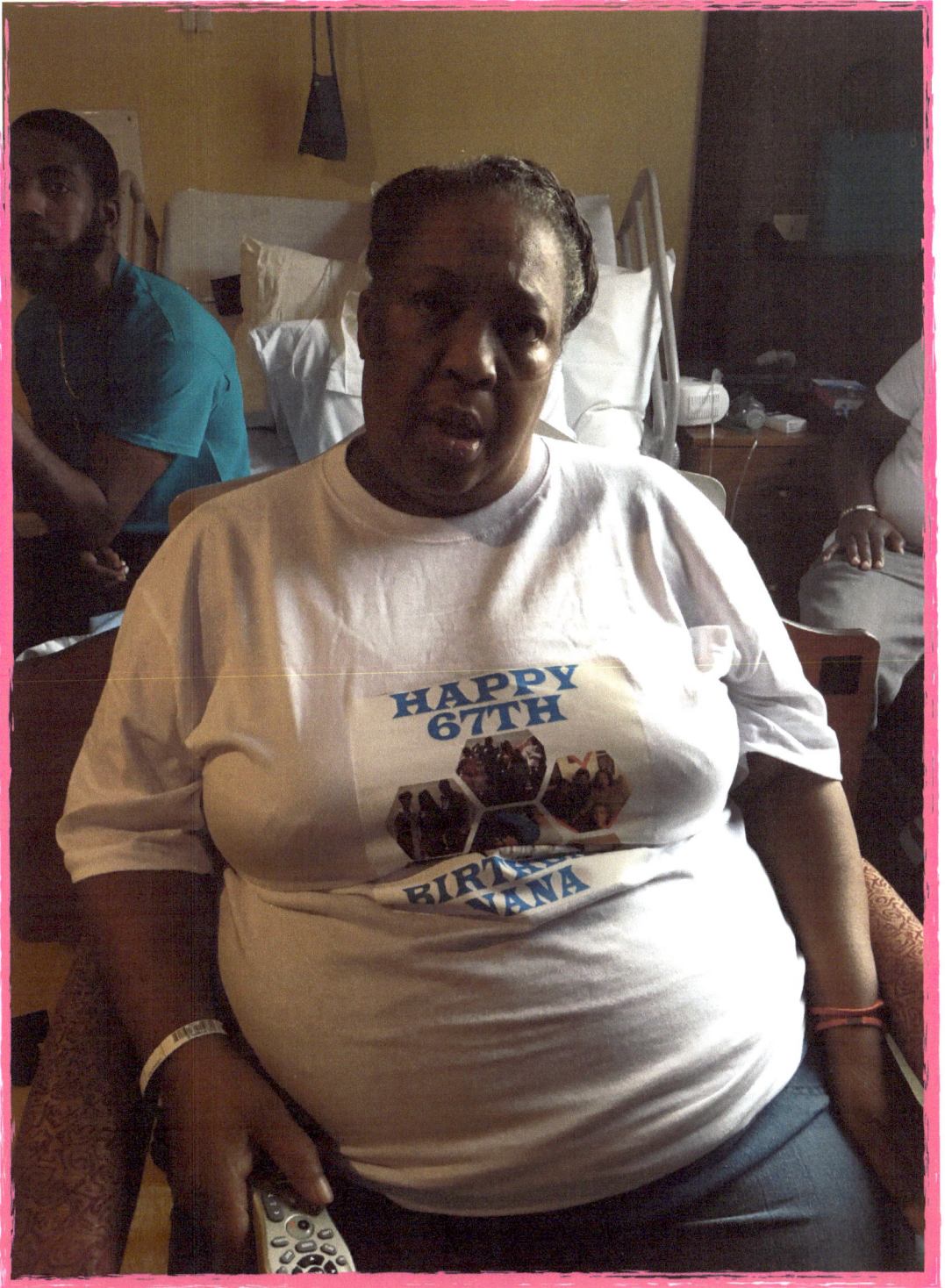

Eldora
Dalrymple

I LOVE THE OCEAN WATER
BECAUSE OF YOU
MILES AND MILES OF WATER
THAT GLISTEN FROM THE SKY OF BLUE
IT REFLECTS FROM LIGHT AND THE MOON
EVERY SECOND I WOULD TAKE
A PICTURE IF I COULD
YOU WOULD LAUGH AT ME ON OUR ROAD TRIPS
CAUSE EVERY TIME WE WOULD PASS WATER
I WOULD TELL THE BOYS
YOU STARTED TO MIMIC AND LAUGH AND
SAY "LOOK AT THE WATER, LOOK AT THE WATER"
MOM I KNOW YOU STILL WATCH AND LISTEN
AS I CAPTURE MY MOMENTS OF PEACE
AND SANITY AT THE WATER
MEDITATING TO GET IN TUNE WITH YOU,
GRANDDADDY, WOOG AND LEGEND
THE SPIRITUAL VIBRATION AND ENERGY
OF THE LOVE ONES WHO HAVE PHYSICALLY DEPARTED

A MOTHERS LOVE

A MOTHERS LOVE IS UNDENIABLE
A MOTHERS LOVE IS INDISPENSABLE
I WOULD BE DOING THE WORLD A DISSERVICE
BY NOT CONTINUING WHAT I STARTED ...
MY MOTHER WOULD NOT WANT ME TO GIVE UP
ON ANYTHING I HAVE CREATED OR STARTED TO BUILD.
I WAS VERY SICK AS A CHILD
AND MY MOM WAS ALWAYS ALWAYS ALWAYS THERE
FROM THE DELIVERY ROOM OF MY TWO OLDEST SONS.
I REMEMBERED AS A CHILD HER NOT EATING
(WHICH WAS HUGE FOR HER)
JUST BECAUSE I COULDN'T EAT.
BECAUSE OF TEST AFTER TEST
TRYING TO FIND OUT WHAT'S WRONG WITH ME
SO IN RETURN I HAD TO BE THERE FOR HER
TEST AFTER TEST
UNTIL GOD TOLD HER SUFFER NO MORE HIS CHILD
I KNOW SHE WAS JOINED BACK WITH HER PARENTS,
SIBLINGS AND HOST OF FAMILY AND FRIENDSHIPS
MOM THIS AND SO MUCH MORE IS FOR YOU
MOM YOU KNEW THAT I WOULD DO ANYTHING FOR YOU
MOM, YOU WOULD OFTEN REQUIRE MY ATTENTION
AS A CHILD OF MINE
AND SHE KNEW HOW TO GET IT
FOR AS LONG AS I CAN REMEMBER
MY MOM HAD BECOME MY OLDEST BABY
MY MOM HOPED AND PRAYED
LOVE, PEACE AND HAPPINESS FOR EVERYONE
I SHALL HONOR AND CHERISH HER MEMORY

MY MOM HAS STYLE

MY MOM IS BEAUTIFUL AND A MOM FULL OF STYLE

MY MOM IS LIVELY WITH A BEAUTIFUL SMILE
MY MOM COULD HAVE BEEN A MODEL,
YES BABY GIRL IS FINE

SHE IS PECAN TAN WITH LIVELY HAIR
SHE IS MIXED WITH CHEROKEE INDIAN

MY MOM LIT UP A ROOM
FROM WHEREVER SHE WOULD STAND
MY MOM SAID SHE HAD A BODY
THAT MADE OTHERS MAD

MY MOM HAS SO MUCH SYTLE FROM HER MAKEUP &
HAIR, HER CLOTHES, SHOES AND BAGS
I CAN NEVER FORGET HOW BEAUTIFUL YOU ARE
ALL I KEPT SAYING IS MAKE SURE
MY MOM LOOKS BEAUTIFUL
MY MOM WAS PLEASED THAT DAY, AS YOU FELT
HER SPIRIT AND THE LORDS TRUMPETS
PLAYED LOUD FOR ALL COULD HEAR.

<u>MY BEAUTIFUL MOM</u>

MY MOM IS BEAUTIFUL &
AN ENERGIZED SPIRIT
SHE IS A WONDERFUL
& PHENOMENAL WOMAN

MY MOM WAS & STILL IS THE
BEST MOM SHE COULD BE
MY MOM IS A SOULFUL WOMAN
WITH FAITH AND GRACE

MY MOM WAS FILLED WITH
WORSHIP AND PRAISE

MY MOM IS A JOYFUL WOMAN WITH
A BOUNTY OF ELEGANCE

MY MOM IS A MAGNIFICENT
WOMAN WITH STYLE
AND A SHINE THAT FILLED HER FACE

MY MOM WAS AND WILL ALWAYS BE
SPECIAL IN HER ARMS IS WHERE I FELT SAFE
MOM YOU KNOW THAT NO ONE WILL
EVER BE ABLE TO TAKE YOUR PLACE.

CONVERSATIONS WITH MY MOM...

HOLIDAYS WILL NEVER BE THE SAME
WE WILL STILL COME TOGETHER AS GOD ALLOWS
BRINGING LOVE AND PEACE

WITH COOKING AND PRAISE,
LISTENING TO MUSIC, LAUGHING AND SINGING
THE ABSENCE OF YOUR VOICE
IT TAKES AWAY PEACE

I SMILE AND YES I STILL SHED TEARS OFTEN
I RANDOMLY SPEAK TO YOU TO TRY TO GET THROUGH IT

WE ALL SPEAK OF YOU OFTEN NOT JUST
DURING THE HOLIDAY SEASON
YOUR LOVE FOR US IS THE PURE REASON

YOU LOVED US UNCONDITIONALLY AND
DID WHATEVER YOU COULD TO CARE FOR US
YOU MADE ONE OF THE BIGGEST CHANGES IN YOUR LIFE
WHEN YOU LEFT BEHIND A PIECE OF THE WORLD
THAT KEPT YOU OUT AT NIGHT

I AM SO THANKFUL THAT, THE BOYS, ZILL AND I
SPENT THE LAST FEW HOLIDAYS WITH YOU
COOKING AND EATING WHICH IS NOW
ONE OF MY FAVORITE THINGS TO DO

CONVERSATIONS WITH MY MOM...

WE REMEMBER WHAT YOU TAUGHT US
AS WELL AS WHAT YOU TOLD US
I KNOW THAT I AM BECOMING MORE LIKE YOU

MESSING UP NAMES TO UNCONTROLLABLY EATING ICE
CARING HEAVILY FOR OUR PLANTS

MOM THEY ARE SO NICE
EVEN THE ONES AT YOUR HOUSE
WE KNOW THAT IS YOU SHINING YOUR LIGHT

I REPEAT YOUR WORDS AND SAYINGS
GOOD AND BAD, AND NEVER FORGET
HOW MANY TIMES WE HEARD YOU PRAYING

PLEASE CONTINUE TO PRAY FOR US
OUR PRAYING ANGEL
GUIDING AND LOVING US TO NO END

HOLIDAYS AS WE KNOW IT ARE DIFFERENT WITHOUT
OUR MOTHER AND OUR NANA
YOUR PRESENCE WILL ALWAYS BE FELT
CAUSE WE KNOW YOU ARE ALL AROUND US

WE NEED YOUR LOVE AND COMFORT
AND PRECIOUS SPIRIT WITHIN US

YOU ARE OUR ANGEL EVERYDAY AND
SWEETLY ON HOLIDAYS

CONVERSATIONS WITH MY MOM...

MOM I THINK ABOUT YOU EVERYDAY
I MISS YOUR PHYSICAL PRESENCE

I TALK ABOUT YOU ALL THE TIME
SOMETIMES I LAUGH AND SOMETIMES I CRY

YOU WILL BE WITH ME IN MY DREAMS
SO I WILL ALWAYS KEEP YOUR SPIRIT ALIVE
SO MANY TIMES I NEEDED YOU AND
YOU WERE RIGHT BY MY SIDE

THE OTHER DAY WHEN WE TALKED YOU TOLD ME
THAT EVERYTHING WILL BE OK

BUT I KNOW YOU FEEL, THAT I AM NOT FINE
YOU SEE HOW MUCH I MISS YOU

I WAS TOLD A COUPLE MONTHS AGO
THAT YOU WERE WORRIED ABOUT ME

YOU TOLD ME YOURSELF, WHEN WE SPOKE LAST WEEK

I AM SO HAPPY THAT I CAN STILL TALK TO YOU
OUR SPIRITS WILL ALWAYS BE CONNECTED

YOU ARE ONLY MISSING FROM THE PHYSICAL
AND THAT MEANS YOU DID NOT DIE

MOM I LOVE YOU SO MUCH,
BEING PRESENT WITH THE LORD
IS A FEELING OF A DIFFERENT OVER JOY
SO THAT I NEVER HAVE TO LET YOU GO

MY MOM, A LEGEND

MY MOM WAS THERE THROUGH ALL MY PAIN
I COULD HERE HER PRAYING TO GOD TO TAKE IT AWAY

MY MOM WAS THERE THROUGH MY TRIALS
I COULD HERE HER PRAYING MAKE IT CEASE

MY MOM WAS THERE THROUGH MY TEARS
I COULD HEAR HER PRAYING TO GOD TO PLEASE DRY MY EYES

MY MOM DIDN'T LEAVE MY SIDE
I AM SO THANKFUL THAT THOSE TIMES I WAS NOT ALONE

SHE WAS THERE WHEN I WAS HAPPY AND JOINED
IN ON THE LAUGHTER

SHE WAS THERE AS I GREW, AND THAT WAS SOMETHING.
SHE WAS THERE BY MY SIDE AS I COOKED

MOM TAUGHT ME HOW TO LIVE AND
SHOWED ME WHAT NOT TO DO

SHE PREPARED ME FOR A LIFE THAT I NEVER KNEW

MY MOM WAS MORE THAN A MOTHER
SHE WAS THE FRIEND AND COMFORTER THAT
BLESSED MY LIFE

SHE MOTIVATED AND SUPPORTED ME WITH
AN UNCONDITIONAL LOVE
THAT ONLY A MOTHER CAN OFFER

YOUR FAITH

EVERYONE KNEW THE TURNUP, BUST DOWN
FUNNY, LET YOU KNOW FIG WITH CLASS

BUT YOU WERE RELIGIOUS TURNED SPIRITUAL
ALWAYS PAYING ATTENTION IN CHURCH
AND UNDERSTOOD THE NEW TESTAMENT

I THANK YOU FOR ALL THE SUNDAYS
THAT YOU TOOK US TO CHURCH
FOR ALL OF THE STORIES OF HOW YOUR AUNTIES
HAD YOU AND YOUR SIBLINGS IN CHURCH

MOM ONE THING I KNOW YOU LOVED MORE THAN
EATING WAS YOUR GOSPEL MUSIC,
THE COLLECTION THAT CAN CHANGE LIVES AND
I AM THANKFUL FOR YOURS, NO MATTER WHAT
YOU WAS GOING THROUGH OR DOING
YOU PLAYED YOUR GOSPEL MUSIC

A FEW OF YOUR FAVORITE SONGS WE ALL KEEP
CLOSE TO OUR HEARTS ANYTIME I WANT TO BE
EVEN CLOSER TO YOU, I PLAY YOUR FAVORITE PART

OVER THE PAST FEW YEARS ALL YOU WANTED TO DO
WAS GO TO CHURCH
NO MATTER THE CITY, TOWN, OR STATE YOU WERE IN
YOU JOINED AS A CHURCH MEMBER OR CHURCH FRIEND

YOUR BELIEF IN GOD CAN NOT EVER MAKE
MY BELIEF IN JESUS STRAY

IM SO GLAD FOR THE TEACHING AND UP
BRINGING OF ALL THAT HE IS
REASSURES ME THAT I GET TO SEE MY MOM AGAIN.

MY HEART

LORD PLEASE MEND MY HEART BACK
IT HAS FALLEN INTO SO MANY PIECES

LORD PLEASE RESTORE MY STRENGTH
THESE LOSSES HAVE MADE ME WEAK
LORD OPEN MY EYES AGAIN
SO THAT MY PATH WILL BE BRIGHT

LORD WORK ON ME SO THAT
I CAN ENDURE THE TRIALS OF THIS PHYSICAL LIFE
LORD MY MIND, KEEP SANE SO THAT
I WILL ALWAYS REMEMBER YOUR WAY

LORD MY HANDS YOU HAVE MADE TO HEAL
AND MY TONGUE TO SPEAK TRUTH
KEEP GIVING ME THE WORD TO SPEAK TRUTH
AND THE HANDS TO TOUCH

THIS WORLD IS FILLED WITH DESPAIR,
DISAPPOINTMENT AND DISBELIEF
SO EMPOWER ME TO BE THE DIFFERENCE OF A
PRAYER WARRIOR, PROMISING SPIRIT,
AND ABUNDANT PROSPERITY

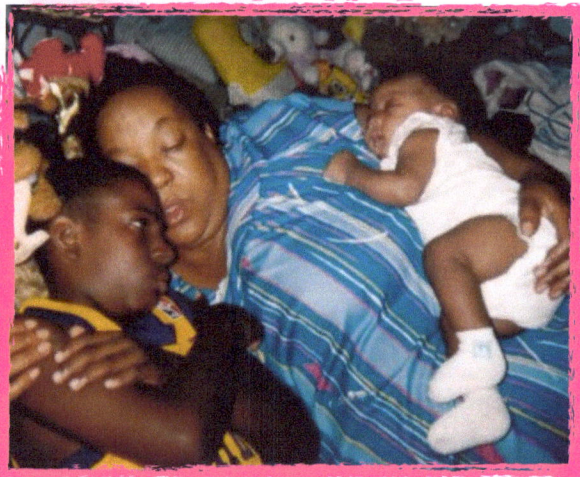

<u>MISSING YOU</u>

MOM YOU KNOW THAT I MISS YOU
EVERYTHING ABOUT YOU

ONE OF THE SADDEST FEELINGS I KNOW
WAS TO SEE YOUR PHYSICAL GO

MOM YOU KNOW HOW I LOVE YOU AND
NEVER WANTED TO SEE YOU HURTING

I WANTED TO GIVE YOU EVERYTHING LIKE
YOU WERE A BIRTH OF MINE

ME GIVING LIFE TO YOU, SOMETHING
WE WOULD JOKE ABOUT YOU BEING MY CHILD
BUT YOU KNOW THAT YOU WERE AND
AS I WAS WILLING OR ABLE

TO DO ALL THAT YOU ASKED ME
& SO MUCH MORE
YOUR PHYSICAL ABSENCE HAS LEFT AN
UN REFILLABLE VOID

I LOVE YOU MOM

<u>GROWING OLD JUST GETTING OLDER</u>

MOM I WATCHED YOU GET OLDER OVER TIME
AND YOU AGED GRACEFULLY LIKE FINE WINE
YOUR BODY MAY HAVE BEEN ILL
ASIDE FROM THAT YOU WERE FINE

WE ALL FORGET THINGS THAT'S JUST A PART OF LIFE
I BET NOBODY COULDN'T GET ANYTHING OVER ON YOU
NANA BE READY TO FIGHT.
YOUR BROTHER CHESTER CONNIE JEROME COOPER
WOULD SAY "YOU SHARP TIGER"

NO MATTER WHERE YOU WOULD GO
EVEN IN YOUR OWN HOME
YOU WOULD HIDE YOUR POCKETBOOK FROM YOURSELF
THE FUNNIEST PART IS WHEN YOU WOULD HIDE
IT FROM YOURSELF AND ASK US WHAT YOU DID WITH IT
WHEN IT CAME TO LENDING MONEY YOU WAS A
BOOKIE WITH A PEN AND YOUR SLIP

MOM YOU MADE US LAUGH MORE THAN YOU MADE US CRY
I TOOK YOU EVERYWHERE WITH ME AND THE BOYS
EVERY TIME I COULD AND YOU ENJOYED IT ALL
THANKFUL THAT I GOT THE CHANCE TO TAKE YOU PLACES
THAT WAS SPECIAL AND I NEVER REALIZED WHAT THAT
MEANT TO US

EVEN IF IT WAS AROUND THE CORNER YOU WOULD
GIVE ME THAT LOOK LIKE MEK MEK
MOMMA WANNA GO AND WE WAS OUT

<u>BEAUTY</u>

MOM I HAVE SO MANY MEMORIES OF YOU
AND I CAN ONLY PRAY THAT YOU ARE AT PEACE
YOU HAD AN UNDENIABLE GLOW ABOUT YOU.
SO HAPPY, SO BEAUTIFUL

I CAN REMEMBER TIMES YOU USING YOUR
SKIN SO SOFT AND AVON
YOUR RED DOOR, YOUR FOUNDATION AND
YOUR LIP STICK

YOUR PRETTY DRESSES AND PANT SUITS.
MY MOM KNEW SHE WAS CUTE
I JUST HAD TO, HAD TO
WRITE A BOOK ABOUT YOU.
I REMEMBER YOU GETTING DRESSED
WITH YOUR HIGH HEELS
YOU HAD A HUNDRED PAIR.
I REMEMBER YOUR CLOSETS AND YOUR
WARDROBES YOU STAYED DRESSED TO KILL
MOM YOU STAYED SNATCHED TO THE TEE
YOU WAS DEFINITELY SOMETHING TO SEE
YOU COULD ROCK YOUR SHADES OR YOUR
GLASSES YOUR HATS AND POCKETBOOKS
A COAT FOR EVERY SEASON

YOU ARE OUR BEAUTY QUEEN, AN EMPRESS
A GODDESS, MY MOM THE MOST BEAUTIFUL BEING

ELDORA FIG DALRYMPLE

I HAVE MEMORIES AS EARLY AS PARKWAY BLVD., WYANDANCH, NY,
AND AS I DON'T KNOW WHAT AGE I WAS. AS I REMEMBER MY MOM
WORKING, I REMEMBER WAKING UP AT NIGHT TO THE SOUND OF
THE HONEYMOONERS THEME SONG, HAPPY THAT THE SOUND I WAS
HEARING, MEANT MY MOM IS HOME.

THE GLIMPSES OF THE LIVING ROOM, THE KITCHEN AND THE
STORY THAT MY MOM LOVED TO TELL. THE STORY OF HOW MY
DAD'S FATHER CAME OVER TO VISIT ONE DAY AND HE WENT TO
PICK ME UP CALLING ME POOH, MY MOM SAID "I POINTED FOR MY
GRANDPA TO GIVE ME WHAT WAS ON TOP OF THE REFRIGERATOR".
AFTER MY GRANDPA SEEN WHAT IT WAS, I HAVE NO IDEA OF
WHAT HAPPENED NEXT AS MY MOM FINISHED THE STORY SHE SAID
"IT WAS HER MARIJUANA TRAY, THAT SHE HAD JUST FINISH
ORDERING TO BE PLACED ON TOP OF THE REFRIGERATOR,
AS THEY SEEN HIM APPROACHING.

AS WE GROW OLDER, MEMORIES BEGAN TO FADE,
HAPPY MEMORIES PROTECTS WITH LOVE,
OTHERS MEMORIES ARE SUPPRESSED WHICH CAN HURT YOU.
NEVER BE AFRAID TO TALK TO SOMEONE YOU TRUST AND PRAY -
MENTAL ILLNESS IS SERIOUS AND I WHEN I SUFFERED AT MY WORST
I HAD TO SEEK PROFESSIONAL GUIDANCE -THA

A MEMORY I SUPPRESSED FOR MANY YEARS WITH A HOST OF OTHERS, LEADS BACK TO MY MOM. I REMEMBER ONE OF MY GRADUATION CEREMONIES AND LEAVING MILTON L OLIVE MIDDLE SCHOOL AND TRAVELING DOWN JAMAICA AVENUE IN MY MOMS BLUE NOVA. I REMEMBER MY MOM SAYING SHE COULDN'T STOP AND THE SUCCINCT VISIONS WERE THAT GRAY HOUSE ON THE CORNER OF JAMAICA AVENUE AND SOUTH 29TH STREETS (GO FIGURE), BUT SADLY MY MOM, MY MOM HAD BEEN KNOCKED UNCONSCIOUS AFTER US HITTING AND SCRAPPING THE SIDE OF THE HOUSE AS SHE MUST HAVE TRIED TO AVOID A COMPLETE DIRECT HIT. I REMEMBER CALLING MY MOM REPEATEDLY CALLING MY MOM, I CAN FEEL THE ANXIETY OF MY YOUNG SELF, WANTING MY MOM TO WAKE UP. THE NEXT THING I REMEMBER WAS MY GRANDPA JOHN, MY MOMS FATHER WAS THERE. HOW DID HE KNOW, WHO CALLED HIM; I HAVEN'T A CLUE BUT THAT'S HIM,
ALWAYS THERE TO FIX EVERYONE ELSE'S PROBLEMS.

I HAVE ALWAYS BEEN CONNECTED TO THE MEN IN MY FAMILIES AND AS I SIT AND REFLECT ON MY LIFE, I NOW UNDERSTAND HOW INSTRUMENTAL THEY HAVE BEEN IN MY LIFE FROM DAY ONE.

WE LIVED IN A NUMBER OF HOMES, STRETCHED ALL OVER OUR SMALL, BUT VERY ACTION FILLED TOWN, AT TIMES RECEIVING GOVERNMENT ASSISTANCE, EMERGENCY HOUSING, HOLIDAY BASKETS AND FREE FOOD FROM THE CHURCH AT THE CORNER OF BLOCK, SOUTH 22ND STREET. MY MOM ALWAYS CLOTHED ME IN A DRESS. I DO NOT KNOW HOW TO EXPLAIN THAT SHE DRESSED ME SO GIRLY THAT WHEN I ARRIVED

IN MIDDLE SCHOOL, I HAD DEFINITELY BECAME A TOMBOY,
ALL THE WAY TO THE EXTINCT OF WEARING DRESS PANTS TO
MY HIGH SCHOOL GRADUATION.
MY MOM WAS NOT HAPPY WITH THAT, SHE TRIED HER BEST TO
GET ME IN A DRESS. I KINDLY HAD TO EXPLAIN, "MOM YOU HAD YOUR
DAYS OF PUTTING ME IN DRESSES". I AM NOT SURE IF MY MOM EVER GOT
OVER ME WEARING PANTS ON THAT BIG DAY. THAT YEAR I
CELEBRATED GRADUATING FROM HIGH SCHOOL AND THE BIRTH OF MY
FIRST SON. JOHLEEK BECAME HER BABY A BABY THAT SHE COULD GIVE
BACK TO ME WHEN SHE WANTED.

I HAVE BEEN VERY FORTUNATE TO HAVE A MOTHER. A MOTHER
WHO ADVISED ME ON HOW TO BE THE BEST PERSON I CAN BE, TO
THE BEST OF HER ABILITY. MY MOM WAS VERY VOCAL IN GETTING
AN EDUCATION AND WORKING. MY MOM SAID I WALKED, TALKED,
READ AND WROTE AT A VERY EARLY AGE. SHE SAID THAT THEY
WANTED TO PLACE ME AHEAD A GRADE AROUND KINDERGARTEN/1ST
GRADE BUT SHE WOULD ALLOW THEM TO. AS I GOT OLDER AND
UNDERSTOOD WHAT SHE WAS SAYING I WAS ELATED. I DIDN'T
UNDERSTAND WHY SHE WOULDN'T LET THEM SKIP ME TO NEXT
GRADE LEVEL, BUT CLASS OF 1996 IT IS. I ALSO HELD THAT
OPPORTUNITY CLOSE TO MY VALUES OF SCHOOL AND LEARNING.
I ALWAYS WANTED TO BE GENIUS. THE FUNNY THING IS,
WHEN I FOUND OUT HOW TO SPELL IT
I WAS LIKE THIS CAN'T BE RIGHT, THIS IS NOT THE CORRECT
SOUND PRONUNCIATION FOR THOSE LETTERS.
EVEN WORST, I STILL DO THAT WITH WORDS TO THIS DAY.

"GET YOUR EDUCATION" - JOHN W. DALRYMPLE

MY MOM WOULD ALWAYS SAY "MY BABY IS SMART", UNTIL SHE GOT MAD AT SOME SILLY I DID. (JUST BECAUSE YOU SMART THAT DOESN'T MEAN YOU DON'T DO SILLY THINGS). MY MOM WOULD SAY "YOU SO SMART YOU D$&B, AND REFERENCE ONE OF HER SIBLINGS SAYING THE SAME, BUT IN MY HEAD I'M LIKE WELL YOU SAID, "THAT SIBLING IS REALLY REALLY SMART",

SO I DON'T KNOW WHAT DUMB MEANS.

THE CONVERSATIONS AND THE QUICK RESPONSES WOULD
BE SOME OF THE FUNNIEST COMBINATIONS OF WORDS.
THAT MY MOM WOULD USE AND BE SERIOUS, ONE OF HER
MOST LOVABLE TRAITS. WE WOULD BE IN TEARS LAUGHING AT
THE THINGS MY MOM WOULD SAY.
IT'S NO SECRET THAT MY MOM LOVED TO EAT, LOOK VERY CUTE
AND HAVE HERSELF A GOOD TIME. SHE MAY HAVE SPENT TIME OUTSIDE
OF THE HOME ENJOYING HERSELF, BUT SHE ALSO ENJOYED HERSELF
WITH HER FAMILY AND FRIENDS AT HOME. IT'S NOT TOO MANY
HOMES THAT SHE AND I SHARED TOGETHER, THAT DIDN'T
BECOME A SAFE HAVEN, A RESTAURANT OR A COMFORT END.
THOSE ARE THINGS THAT SHE DID AS A WOMAN OF GOD.

WE ALL FALL SHORT AND EVEN FALL DOWN AT TIMES;
BUT THERE IS NOT ANYTHING LIKE GRACE AND MERCY - THA

MY MOM HAS CARED FOR ME IN MY WEAKEST TIMES.
I HAVE BEEN HOSPITALIZED OVER 15 TIMES.
AT THE AGE I BEGAN TO WRITE MY
AUTOBIOGRAPHY, THE NUMBER 15 WAS MORE THAN HALF MY AGE.
MY MOTHER WAS THERE EVERY TIME, IT WOULD BE TIMES THAT
I COULD NOT EAT SHE DEPRIVED HER SELF FROM EATING TOO.
I KNEW SHE WOULD BE HUNGRY.
MY MOM LOVE TO EAT AND SHE WASN'T DOWN FOR SKIPPING A MEAL.

I LOVE MY MOM, MY MOM ALSO WITNESSED THE BIRTH OF MY TWO

OLDEST SONS. AFTER THE FIRST TIME WHO WOULD WANT

TO SEE THAT AGAIN. I LIVED WITH MY MOM UNTIL THE AGE OF 26.

SO YOU COULD SAY I WAS A BRAT, AS OF A MATTER FACT, I SLEPT IN

MY MOM'S BED UNTIL THE AGE OF 18. THAT'S AROUND THE SAME TIME

I GAVE BIRTH TO MY FIRST SON AND OF COURSE SHE

KICKS ME OUT OF HER BED.

I HAD A VERY BAD PREGNANCY, I STAYED AROUND
MY MOM AS MUCH AS I COULD.
I LOST MY UNCLE WHICH IS MY MOTHERS BROTHER AND MY
GRANDFATHER WHICH IS MY MOTHER'S FATHER IN 1995, WHILE MY SISTER
AND I WAS BOTH PREGNANT WITH OUR OLDEST SONS. WE REALLY NEEDED
EACH OTHER, TRAVELING I95 FROM NEW YORK TO NORTH CAROLINA AND
BACK AGAIN. WHICH IS A PART OF MY MOMS NORMAL ROUTINE.

MY MOM LOVED THE STATE OF NORTH CAROLINA, SHE LOVED
THE STATE SO MUCH SHE MOVED BACK AND FORTH EVERY FEW YEARS.
I THINK SHE ENJOYED KNOWING THAT SHE COULD
MOVE TO NORTH CAROLINA WHEN SHE WANTED AND BACK TO
NEW YORK WHEN SHE PLEASED.

IT SEEMED AS IF SHE MOVED EVERY TWO YEARS, LIKE IT WAS
MANDATORY. SHE TRIED TO LEAVE ME BEHIND A COUPLE TIMES,
YEAH RIGHT I WAS EITHER THERE WITH BAGS OR GOING TO PACK MY
MOMS BAGS TO MOVE BACK TO NEW YORK. EVERYONE TEASED HER
ABOUT MOVING BACK AND FORTH SO OFTEN.

IT WAS ALSO TIMES THAT PEOPLE WOULD ASK "YA MOMMA
STILL DOWN SOUTH"? MY SISTER AND I WOULD GET SILLY
SOMETIMES AND TELL THEM YEAH, CAUSE NANA WAS PROBABLY ON
HER WAY BACK HOME ANYWAY.

MY MOM WAS VERY DIFFERENT SHE LOVED, BUT SHE WAS A
FIGHTER, SHE WOULD WELCOME YOU IN AND WHEN YOU GOT ON HER
NERVES SHE WOULD PUT YOU OUT. SHE WANTED TO GO WHEREVER
WE WAS HAVING SOMETHING AT AND BE READY TO LEAVE IN A
HEART BEAT AND IF NO ONE WANTED TO
TAKE HER HOME SHE WOULD CALL HER A CAB.

HER SON IN LAW AND I HAVE THING WE CALL THE NANA FACE AND IT IS USUALLY
GIVEN WHEN YOU DON'T VERBALLY SPEAK YOUR RESPONSE BUT THE NANA FACE
SHOWS THE DISGUST OF WHAT THE PERSON SAID.

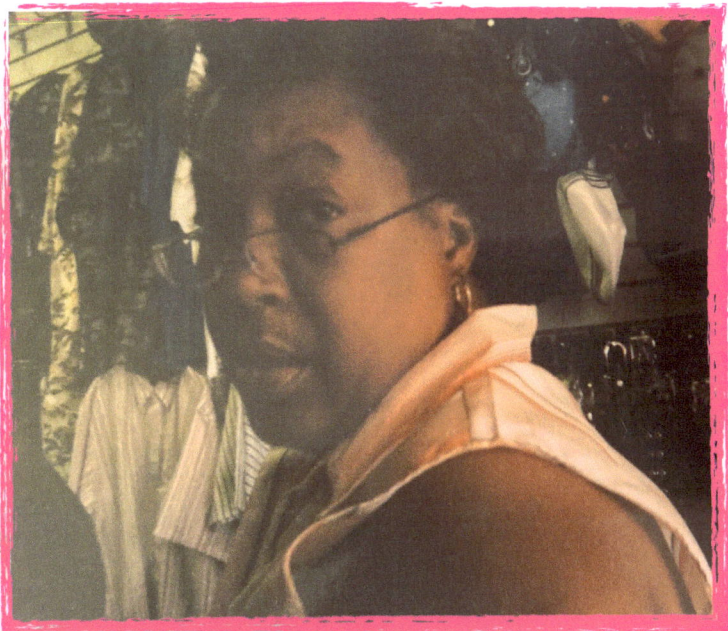

MY MOM, THE COMMUNITY NANA, AUNTY, AND MA, SHE HAD SOMETHING ABOUT HER. SHE MADE A PERSON JUST WANT TO TALK TO HER CAUSE SHE WAS EITHER GONNA CHECK YOU, CRACK A JOKE AND MOST OF HER JOKES WERE X-RATED, GO FIGURE. I NEVER THOUGHT OF CHANGING NEITHER OF MY PARENTS EVEN IN THEIR IMPERFECTIONS.

MY MOM AND I HAD DISAGREEMENTS, MANY OF THEM. I BET ONE THING, I NEVER RAISED MY HAND UP TO HER. WHILE SPEAKING ON A BET, I WOULD DO THIS BOOK A DISSERVICE IF I DIDN'T SPEAK ON MY MOMS LOVE FOR CARD GAMING. MY MOM LOVED TO PLAY POKER, GIN, 5000, SPADES, RUMMY, CRAZY 8, I DECLARE WAR, PITY PAT AND TUNK.

IN THIS IMPERFECT WORLD WE ENJOYED EACH OTHER'S PRESENCE AND LAUGHTER WE HAD MORE FUN THAN ANYONE COULD IMAGINE. I LEARNED TO REALIZE THAT MY MOM HAD A FLARE OF MALICE, THAT HER THREE CHILDREN HAS AS WELL. THANK GOD WE ARE NOT THE WORST OF THE WORST. EVEN IN OUR UPS AND DOWNS LIKE ANY DAUGHTER AND MOTHER WE WERE STILL INSEPARABLE.

SOMETHING THAT I CHERISH YOU ARE MY MOM AND MY FRIEND SO
NO WE DIDN'T AGREE ON EVERYTHING BUT WITH YOUR
FORGIVENESS, YOU MADE ME KNOW THAT THAT
WAS OK ONLY BECAUSE JESUS WAS THE ONLY HUMAN
WHICH WAS PERFECT.   WE WOULD GET UPSET OVER
THINGS THINGS THAT, IF I COULD HAVE YOU BACK.
I WOULD PRACTICE HARD TO NEVER GET UPSET AGAIN.
AT ANYTHING YOU DO OR ANYTHING YOU SAY.
I DECLARED IN MY LIFE THAT ANYTHING OF MALICE
YOU EVER DID HAS BEEN ERASED!

*ELDORA "FIG" DALRYMPLE was born on October 10, 1951
in Lee County, North Carolina
to the late Arnie Bell Young and John Willie Dalrymple Sr.
Eldora lost her mother at a very young age
and was raised by her
mother's two sisters Ada and Jennie Young-Williams.
One of the many things her aunts taught her was
how to cook, in which she mastered.
Eldora attended W. B. Wicker School in North Carolina.*

*In her early teenage years, Eldora would travel from
North Carolina to New York to visit her father before
choosing to make it her home.
Fig continued to cook at her fathers restaurant and
helped at his Fish n Chip. She graduated from
Wyandanch Memorial High School in 1971. Eldora
loved to cheer and was a part of many teams
throughout her school years. She obtained her
Business Degree from Adelphi and later on became a
Mental Hygiene Therapy Aide at Pilgrim State
and Long Island Developmental Center
(LIDC) in building 29.*

*Eldora was raised in church and joined many church families,
becoming an endeared member, wherever her feet landed.
She loved to play her gospel music while she prepared her
Sunday dinners. She would play her music no matter the
circumstances. Even as she loved church
and hearing the Word from God, she was also the
life of any gathering.*

As God gifted her to dance, she did not hesitate to praise
and thank him. Nana loved to dance, she could dance
any one into hiding and taught a few, many moves
including the four corners. Nana loved to make
it roll, with her brother Connie nicknaming her "Jelly Roll".

As she not only loved to cook, she loved to eat as well, which
also led her beloved Father to name her "Fat Fig". Fig was a one
woman catering team, the word spread quickly on how great her
food was and she was asked and hired to cook on many occasions.
Fig lit up any room she entered, she made many of us laugh with
direct statements, sometimes too much information, but also
telling it like it is, what it is, how it is,
how it should be and then some.
She did not exempt anyone from her jokes and very quick replies.
As a mother and a grandmother she was named "NANA".

She kept it more than real and loved each and everyone
of them more than herself.

Nana would go above and beyond for them, she
always made a way. She also kept her daughters in the
kitchen, gifting them with recipe after recipe.

I LOVE YOU, MOM - ONLY GOD KNOWS THE
TRUE ACHE MY HEART HAS -THA

SHE LOVED AND WAS LOVED
BY MANY, OUR QUEEN!

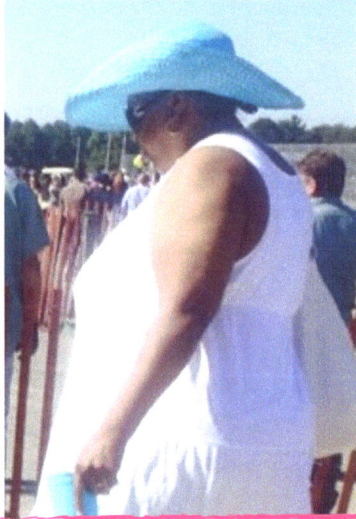

God gave Nana a very extensive family, many families
being joined together for purpose.
She wanted peace, love, and for everyone to be happy.
She welcomed many with love and others with a full plate.
She shared loving and caring words with you.
Keep her close in spirit and her words won't ever part.

I HUMBLY PRAY FOR COMFORT, SANITY,
PEACE AND LOVE TO ALL
WHO HAVE LOSS A CHILD
PARENT OR GRANDPARENT - THA

Tomeka is an inspirational writer, poet and author.
Her latest book entitled "Our Beloved Angel"
Legend Gejaune Tasheem King Arthur is available
on Amazon and on her writer's
website THA.WriteHer.COM

Tomeka holds an AAS in Visual Communications,
BA in Technical Management and
MA in Educational Technology. She
has written for many years and has extensive
experience in the educational, financial, health, and
music industries. Her niche skill sets include
inspirational writing, technology and design.

www.ingramcontent.com/pod-product-compliance
Lightning Source LLC
Chambersburg PA
CBHW041546040426

42447CB00002B/68